TAKE NOTHING WITH YOU

Kuhl House Poets
edited by Mark Levine and Emily Wilson

TAKE NOTHING WITH YOU

Poems by SARAH V. SCHWEIG

UNIVERSITY OF IOWA PRESS, *Iowa City*

University of Iowa Press, Iowa City 52242
Copyright © 2016 by Sarah V. Schweig
www.uiowapress.org
Printed in the United States of America

Design by Barbara Haines

The University of Iowa Press is a member of Green Press Initiative and is committed to preserving natural resources.

Printed on acid-free paper

Library of Congress Cataloging-in-Publication Data
Names: Schweig, Sarah V., author.
Title: Take nothing with you / Sarah V. Schweig.
Description: Iowa City : University of Iowa Press, 2016. | Series: Kuhl House poets
Identifiers: LCCN 2016008378 | ISBN 978-1-60938-457-9 (pbk) |
    ISBN 978-1-60938-458-6 (ebk)
Subjects: | BISAC: POETRY / American / General.
Classification: LCC PS3619.C4927 A6 2016 | DDC 811/.6—dc23
LC record available at https://lccn.loc.gov/2016008378

This book is dedicated to my family, near and far.

Deine Frage—deine Antwort.
Dein Gesang, was weiß er?

Your question—your answer.
Your song, what does it know?

—Paul Celan

Contents

4

I

SUBDIVISIONS

Line up the animals.

Line up the animals we housed
because we could house them.

Line up the animals we loved
behind glass. The parakeets, the mouse,

the cracked-shell tortoise,
three goldfish

with flared fins, opening and closing
their pursed round mouths

at surfaces.
The goldfish bones

we buried in the yard.
Scales sequined the soil.

Line up the wild things.

The mockingbird seeking sky.
The scuttling unseen scorpions.

Cut into the air
their outlines. Line up

the heartless. Line up
the animals. They—

like us—
once lived in this ether.

CONTINGENCIES

Someone in this city calls himself the Latin King.
Kids who break the law are called Delinquents.
The Law is a set of rules, always slightly changing.
To Break is to inflict a kind of change on a thing.
Across the city the Latin King is spray-painting
his pseudonym. Juvenile Delinquents blot it out again.
(Beautification.)

This is a treatise on BLANK.
Had the phrase OFFICES OF RAIN meant anything,
ALL LIGHTS ARE ON IN THE OFFICES OF RAIN
would have suggested that it is raining.
In this treatise, suggestion carries agency.
It is now raining. I am walking through it.
I would like to say AND THEN, but I am merely
continuing. That the rain will end, I'm fairly certain.

The rain has ended. Juvenile Delinquents
enlisted by the city to blank out the sign of the Latin King
are dressed in white smocks. They are kids. Sometimes they are
known as Black or Latino. Today, into white paint, they
dip rollers. I am White and have just been walking through rain.

This is a treatise on BLANK. I would like to include the Idea, sometimes known as Image, of replacing Chandeliers with Lampshades. Two friends make this decision. They resist the perceived opulence of their new house on Hall Street (Gentrification). They turn light on and off by a switch.

This is a treatise on BLANK. Replacing OFFICES OF RAIN with TEMPLE OF STONE, I am breaking this treatise.
TEMPLE OF STONE means something, as I stood in it yesterday.

Juvenile Delinquents have finished repairing harm to the city and have gone home. This city feels empty when it empties even slightly. This could mean Plenitude is a Precondition for the city I call Home.

Yesterday,
in the TEMPLE OF STONE, we were telling stories.
This was the meaning of standing in that building at that time.
The stories were about a man. The Telling of Stories occurred on the occasion of that man entering, suddenly,

BLANK.
What is the meaning of this?
Had I known, I would not have begun it. I am walking through it

to understand. Matter becomes Boy becomes Man becomes
BLANK. This is how I understand it. The city feels empty
because it empties. I would like to say Beauty
where there is a BLANK. I can't. This was a treatise
on Meaning. This is the end of Treatise.

BRIGHTON BEACH

Because the people I love don't believe in heaven
we take the train to Brighton. *Atlantic Avenue, Pacific Street.* The ocean

is always the ocean, so we take the Q. *Seventh Avenue, Prospect Park.*
It's hard to explain. The tide rises, and we drink all the beer we brought.

Before the restaurants, before the boardwalk, crackheads slept in dunes
and girls turned tricks, or so we hear from a guy we met. He grew up here

and for a living now he installs in bars electric chandeliers. In these waves,
when he was young, his sister drowned, and because she's gone

he takes the Q to Brighton. *Church Avenue, Beverly Road.* We don't speak
the language spoken. At a loss to say what we mean, we take the Q

to get there. And because the sun dies in Brighton, we know the day
can end, and because the sky can't help but darken, we go home again

to Boerum Hill. *Cortelyou Road, Avenue J.* In these waves, one night,
one summer, I kissed someone. We walked through sands and bottle glass

so we could touch the ocean the way the water can't help but touch the land,
and in the end we couldn't help but touch, so we took the Q, that year,

to Brighton. I didn't believe in heaven. It's hard to explain. Take the train, touch the sea, walk the sand. *Kings Highway, Sheepshead Bay.*

Along the shore lie those who know there is no heaven, and no answers to our questions, and that ships leaving piers look like distant chandeliers.

EX MACHINA

S, with her Ex, goes out
in Alphabet City to eat
at a place called Ate on 8th.

And as they raise their glinting
red-wine glasses, eyes meet.
Ex says, *To us*, like the past.

Outside, 8th Street bustles
toward the lower Lower
East Side. S averts

her eyes when she feels
overly interior and talks of
the ongoing war, going on

overseas. *When will it end?*
Ex replies: *Those who hate
Democracy hate us for being free,*

and as he talks S recalls
resting her head over his heart
in bed. The sign for infinity

seems an 8 tipped over, or
two S's intertwined, figures
on their sides.

Just then, the waiter
descends: *Everything ok?*
The fare is fine.

KARMA ACADEMY

Blackbirds are blackbirds.
Crows are human. They take issue
with my elocution.

Blackbirds are pussycats.
Crows are dicks. I think
about god like I think

about sex, my bird
in your wallet, pink
and black, hard

to subvert our condition.
It's not a car, but a back-
pack. Not a transport

but a heft. The swifts
dive into, in lieu of smokestack,
your JanSport. The stranger

downstairs hardly works.
His voice roars up
the radiator.

I'm vacant
in my rental, you're
a poet, and when Blanche

LeBlanc says *the fact*
I can do next to nothing
to alleviate the suffering of others,

—even those I do not know
personally!—is more
than I can handle,

I tip two bits
to feather my hair
in a wingback chair.

My cat euphemistic
in gold and black, my crows
collecting glittery trash,

my hair in a knot
held in place with
two pins. The last place

to escape our condition
was in. Blanche LeBlanc
goes on, begs

the blackbirds at dusk
to *please reassign*
whatever is keeping her

vertical. Fuck
the fucking fucker
says the radiator.

BLOODWORK

Some guy, bleeding, just beaten
by hooded strangers on the late train,

asks some girl, a witness, the same question
that lovers ask each other, turning from mirrors:

How do I look? and she, bystanding,
replies: *Frankly, you're in a bad way.*

She'd been thinking of the one,
long gone, who got away, the one

who'd taken himself from her
and those days when she'd turn, adoring,

to him. *Amazing.* (That's what he used to say.)
Thus she, on loss, ruminates.

You can see what she's getting at,
can see where she's heading. Your eyes

have got that same telling
ache and sanguine reverie. You too

have once walked in twos, linked
to another in the light rain . . . .

But we all, now and then, walk alone,
especially in the City of Men,

where most you meet are bled dry
and broken, or have cashed in

care for possession, where the injured
offer you their arms so you might

help them better,
like failures, like lovers,

where the aimless fling curses
like boomerangs through the air . . . .

QUELLE NIGHT

She is, tonight, in spite of.
That's what she said, going out,
locking the door, closing her winter coat
against the cold. She is
in spite of it all.

To hell, she says, *with the weather,*
swaggering to a café on Broadway.
she needs a drink and a novel
project. But how belabored
it all is. All these people

with all their first-world problems
talking over red-eyes, commending
their deadpan deliveries of quips
about Nietzsche and flattering
each other's dry Wittgenstein:

One of the most misleading
representational techniques
in our language is the use of
the word "I." (I see that—
and yet—)

Exhausting, she says. Quelle
night. What are you

searching for? As she strays
back home, the salt trucks salt
the dirt-sick snow:

In spite of, in spite of, in spite—

RED BANK

Deaths came out of the blue and the weather complied.
After, the sound of running water and the girls whose names

are not mentioned. He said my disposition was a fragment. He drove
one-handed. Two rules: No complete lines. A little blood in the water.

SHIFT

We all have our jobs and we do them.
We have our lives and our rented rooms.
We pass through time. We are born with our mouths
open. The glass diminishes, the bartender fills it.
The broken clock, stuck, still ticks.
Sometimes, the day passes easily and we rejoice
at how we've been brought seamlessly
closer to death. We work and sleep until somebody slips. Until
somebody leaves. One thing I've learned, and it still needs work:
The stranger the lights the more arbitrary the lord.

*

He's from South America, so the suits named Sir call him Tequila.
He cleans the marble lobby with Windex. Spritzes, wipes.
Have you seen the trees? is a question that deflects
almost successfully. Without weather, what would we say
to each other? White petals blossom and fall. He whitewashes
the red brick wall. For just how long can a person be treated
like a wounded swan before growing wings to complete this hall's
thankless decoration? In Arlington Cemetery, on New Year's Day,
I watched the outcropping of marble grown suddenly over new graves.

*

Our expectations are tempered now,
like the hard soil where my mother once planted simple flowers,
tamped down. Today, I've decided Beauty can still be found.
Under hung lights, he pours across the spotless floors
a tonic of water and bleach. To chart obstructions is also
a profession, disclosing wreckage on the cruel sea floor.
The German painter goes through the door.
No man is born with mop in hand.
We'll work and sleep until somebody sings.
A woman clutches fistfuls of change.
When the phones ring, my arms lift like wings.

*

All day, by glass doors, Isaiah stands guard, hard of hearing,
bad knees, humming Tchaikovsky. Give a man a square inch plot
of shoddy land and he'll put his whole life there,
he'll put his whole mind there. The German painter paints
ruined temples the way they might have been. There is
no reason. On the street this morning, a bird's severed wing.
Wind blows across an old sun.
I too have tried to move through the world without thinking.

*

Some things we write down so we can forget; others, to bring us back.
There's a song. It goes, *The cloud of ash is coming*
to ruin the corn, to wash away the stalks, to coat the fruit in dust, coming
to blanket the flock, and cover us.
There's a song that goes, *Someday I'll take off, and won't come back.*
Someday I will have been traveling. This, then, to bring me back.

2

ALL THE MASKS

Smelling like bananas was never a thing I wanted.

It's just something that happened. *That's the thing*

about growing up, the man in the banana suit said.

Some people give off the stench of THIS IS

ALL THERE IS. I don't get that sense about

the man in this particular suit. *Today, I will make*

all the masks I can, I tell him. And he says, *Great.*

MIDDLEBURG

Real estate people lived there. My family
grew wealthy, and Father,
Aphrodite's biographer, gave me

a huge grin. Uncle's wasted,
quotes Aristotle. Man is not exactly
horsey. The honeybee

feels a bit mean. Something bad
happened. The three of us eventually
worked out a goodbye.

PRIMORDIAL LIFE

The black cat across the wood floor stretched
into a crescent. The floor's patterns depended on where
each trunk had been amended. The process lent credence to the invention.

Collapse lent credence to materials. Silver, copper.
Don't mistake the personal for lumber or a lumberyard in winter.
Personal Expression is no longer important.

The books I have not yet balanced.
The process is the glitter of circles scattered
across the dark floor of a numbered room wide open.

It seemed the truest thing. Loneliness. I worked hard
to own it. The airport, a nice touch. The airport was the constant
breeze from which I—daughter of some scholar—laughed.

THE SOUND OF RUNNING WATER

Already we see him. Hello. My dad, that loosener, always on the phone,
    listening
to who-for-ever felt to him very akin. Longinus, or his mother. *To the shore!*

That didn't help. He later, I hear, thinks we—the family he tossed off—are
    temporary.
I—a young one—will not finish out the joy of that spring. He had luck.

THE LOVERS

After he left, she darned our clothes, want-not, need,
and needle. We grew and it grew

colder. She shoveled snow. We shoveled. The world too
could vanish, if it so chose, flake white.

Seasons were nothing then but sun-slant and orbit.
They passed. Understand, it was a matter of cheekbone and heirloom,

of rain and doorframe. She sorted through what had not been
taken and who had been taken in. Understand,

she wanted to be a painter. He wanted a wife
and son. After he left, the abandoned piano still hummed

its second-hand sonatas. Lovers still walked winter streets,
adorned in the world and linked miraculously

arm in arm. This is a story about a man and a woman
who met when they were very young.

THE ABANDONMENT

A man I once loved has built a mountain.
You're avoiding something, I say when I've climbed to its crest.
That's a projection, he says, repairing the thatched roof on his modest hut.
You're projecting that I'm projecting, I say, *Because your parents were
    psychoanalysts.*

I sit down in the plastic grass, which he's woven leaf by leaf into the turf.
You're using description of a moment to avoid what's really at hand, he says.
But I live for my art, I say. *I don't have anything else.*
You had me once, he says, *and you still said that.*

When I ask if he would like to go swim in the Lake of Remembrance,
he says, *Don't change the subject.* When I ask what I can do to help, he says,
Here is a shovel. The mountain never brought him happiness. The
    mountain never
brought him peace. *Now we will bury the ash of our teachers.* On this we
    could agree.

LONESOME HEAVEN INTERVAL

Churchman's Crossing's
pill-blue buildings.
AstraZeneca's pill-blue
buildings. This is one

lonesome interval. Now
the veggie chips. Now
the pirates' booty. Don
a pillbox hat with some

panache. Now the coffee.
Now the office parks.
Now the first sip, now the
last. The crocuses shot up

in absence of. Watertown.
Newtown. Blacksburg,
Virginia. Now the signposts
cut like trunks. Now insert,

now delete. Ricki Lake.
Virginia Creeper. You are going
to live forever, and this is one
lonesome interval.

SEHNSUCHT

She's cunt, chest,
cutest, sun-est. She stuns.
He's thus: He's tense, he's uncut, he's
nuts. He hunts. He shuns, he
cusses, he cuts nets, he cuts hens,
hunts. Tense? Tensest, he cuts
suns. Then, thus: He & She.
Thus, the "us" stunt. Shh . . .
He's testes, uncut. He hunts
cunt. He hests. He cuts. Shh . . . . she's
stuc—He cuts & cuts, shuns
& cusses. Then, she hushes. Sun
set. He's shunt. She's thus: Uncunt, un-
chest, unnest, unhitch, un-
sun-ness. She's unsun, she's
unset. Then, she's tense. She tests
tents & such. She tests these nets
& these nets. She tests the hutches,
she tests the huts. *Test the hush nets.*
She tests the hush nets. *The theses?*
Unset, unsent. Sunset, hence, sun
set. He hunts suns, hence, she's
sun-cut. Thus: Hush
hush hush. (She's hush.)

SCHWEIG

We weigh his wishes:
    Ice, chess, hisses.

She eggs his chess.
    I chew his ice.

He sees we.
    He hisses.

She & I eschew
    his hisses.

We see she
    is his. We see I

is his. We weigh
    eggs. He

chews his eggs
    (i.e., we) & he's

high. High, he
    sighs sighs.

*

He chews ice,
    which hisses.

He chesses.
    She sews.

He eschews eggs.
    She sighs.

He hisses ice.
    She weighs eggs.

He wishes eggs,
    ice.

She wishes
    his hisses,

sighs.
    He's ice.

She's sighs.
    (*We is?*

I wish.)

THE AUDIT

Groupwise, busy
search. Start off
your week with
some cake.

Spatula, buy eggs.
Butter your kayak
with cake. Harvard,
Washburn. My girlfriend's

son's graduation
party yesterday.
Blackberry outage. Some
cake. (Investigate.)

Harvard, spatula,
my girlfriend's son's
party yesterday.
Busy search, blackberries.

The audit questions,
investigates the state
of yesterday. Question
the audit. Forkful

of angel. A wise group
of suits, after delays, never

came. Harvard,
margarine. Calling and calling,

today, all the neighbors,
utter undress, complete
disarray, I propped the door
open, which is to say

Washburn, kayak.
I propped my window
with an eyeglass case.
Butter your kayak, cake.

AFTER CATULLUS

Tell the man I loved that this city will not miss him,
how its districts of flowers and painted women,

worthless now, will not grieve him, how the prophets
and palm-readers, how they wander his street empty-handed, indifferent

to the building where he lived, long since derelict,
long gone forbidden. The looters came and left,

crossed bridges with citizens, walked from ill-lit avenues littered
with wineglasses over the river in thousands, leaving town, gorgeous

in falling light, their heads turned down, hauling away
their hoards. When you find the man I loved

languishing in some remote city, screwing woman after
woman, loving none, tell him how I gave the looters all his books

scrawled in dead languages, how I gave them the shoreline,
piers, and river, now engorged with drowned horses still hitched

to carriages, gave them the evenings we spent, and the year,
and the ferries that took tourists homesick into distances,

how I gave away the night, those dark sails filled with stars
hoisted into the sky above the West Side, and how

I gave them the stars, and how I gave them the West Side.
When you find the man I loved, tell him to fathom

these dismal rooflines, this bereft horizon, our views
long gone, and to imagine me, the woman he once loved, the last

one left, now sleeping nights in cut flowers,
dismantling by day all our tired violins.

TO A DAUGHTER

I raise a glass to you, Lorraine, to your nonexistence.
In the dark, I pour a glass and raise it up.

The golden strip beneath the door tonight
means the light's left on in the hall,

the man who would have been your
father has been drinking quietly the dark alcohol.

Sometimes, he speaks. He said nothing yesterday.
An innocent man was killed by the government

so he drank, and I watched a boy by the river
catch a brilliant fish. He held it up for his father to see.

It wriggled in the air for water, like a prize or kept
promise, then went still. Life left it, you see, and it was better.

And the boy gutted the fish with a slight and silver
blade, like his father. And they raised their hands up,

glistening with scales, and the scales were the colors of rain.
In squares, fountains run, pointless and without cease.

This is what his thirst is like, your father, this is like his pain.
You've been spared, my daughter, but he carries the light, Lorraine.

Tonight, I watch him, the man who would have been.
He raises a glass and, like light sudden through drapes,

it breaks, the way a promise might, and so he takes
straight from the bottle a long drink. *Cheers to you*, I say.

I am no one's mother. I look at my life as a long hallway
no one enters, a slight but gleaming space. It's better.

All day, fountains run driven by some obscure
need. The boy discarded small bones in one, like a tired god.

See the boy. See the fish he caught, his father grilling it.
It glimmers and chars the way the night does.

The night says something sometimes, but knew better
today. I pour one out, and another. Tonight,

in our house, all lights turn on and beam out
and in heavy downpours fountains run absurdly.

Tonight, the boy will taste the charred fish, the brilliant
city you'll never see, and the men who are dead

will still be dead tomorrow and the streets will go on,
like your father, speechlessly. He takes a long drink,

and is better. He carries with him what light
there is, and long ago, he ignited something

beneath my skin, or in my bones. It burns, like want,
like pain. You've been spared, Lorraine, the dark

and what light there is to break through rain.
You've been spared the man

who would have been, and spared the girl
who loved him without question, without cease.

You see, the light is what she thought he carried,
but it was only his thirst, all along, only his pain.

He pours one out for you, just now, his daughter.
We raise it up to you, Lorraine.

3

ROOMS

Sometimes I climb a dark building,
a high stack of studios, LET-ON-LEASE, and I can see

how the world breathes, how oxygen is just so
easy.

My life is
a slow rotation, a constant relocation

from one empty room to another where
multicolored lights hang

from the ceiling, hung
with hundreds of tiny, clear tacks. In each room,

a martyr, each martyr moving from one
empty room to another.

Here,
above this bulb-draped city, missing

a once-lover's empty arms, calloused hands, eyelids
when he slept, I see,

by the freeway, the glass motel.

It flashes VACANCY.

Stars are windows in the sky.
God is moving through each room

searching for something, while
in every direction, the universe recedes from his touch.

(You would refuse to turn on the lights.)

Once, we'd wake
in yellow dawn-light, our bodies

tangled, your bedroom, the window open, the cold come in.

At the bottom of the ocean, unreached by waves
of light, there is no weather. Instead (so I've heard),

a perfect species of albino fish
never comprehends the concept *Surface*.

All night, insects skim the water. Inside stilted beachside houses,
roaches scatter. This was our vacation.

The viridian sea of grasses washed ashore to the white sand.
We touched them, I sliced my fingers, I scarred souvenirs

onto my curious hands.

This was our vacation.

The storm rolled in after the Blue Rain.

It snuffed out cadmium ends of cigarettes
pointellating the cityscape, neon

from signs up and down Rain Street,
and rising water erased

eyes from every picture frame.
In this life,

people take trips, open windows,
dislocate,

take photos, and return home.

This morning, I woke before you woke, tore poems
from my notebook,

folded pages
into swans, arranged them

on your nightstand in ink-scarred pairs,
and let them

float. This morning,

I woke before you woke. I left before you left. This morning, I saw
how people emerge into daylight. Today, in this city,

there was some kind of celebration.
People emerged for the preparations.

This morning was the Blue-Ballooned Morning
anchored to the earth. This morning, the world turned out

to consist of just glass objects.
Then, today, we became

Blue Rain.

You've told me already about your UMBRELLA CRUSADES.
What else is there to say?

We used to sugar-lift our eyes

to look for the stars in a smogged-up sky,
for our voices in sifted mists between stacks of offices, for

workers, pigment-dyed, leaving factories where, every day,
in just four colors, they silkscreen

this Godless World.

Now, on the roof, a clear night, a dark high
building, satellites, stars, and radio towers seem

equidistant. Red lights breathe in the night.
At that moment you and I were

of this Junksick World.

The only art left on Earth is the slow, patient study and meticulous
enumeration of suffering. I keep a tally on my wall.

And in the violet thunder of an early summer

storm one night, after glass drinks dislocated, emptied
into my fast, my body, a woman held me up

in rain. We saw how easily streams
washed, pink-petalled, through gutters on side streets and into

the steel arteries of the city. We brimmed

with pearly gin, each lightning strike struck the sky
in shades of knowing, of unknowing—

All around us a split-second split—

emergency

lights—fluorescent stars—in all the buildings

went out.

No one

could forecast the storm.

The hawks, like prayers, emerged and began their slow circles
above.

Early on a Tuesday morning, when the sea released
a thousand tiny black pearls, I rose

from sea-grass,
buoyed to the surface in the middle of my sleeping, woke

to a roomful of wilting magnolia
dreams from the night before. Still

damp, the sad dozens of petals spelled the euphorics
of pain across the floor, the linguistics of stillness after

the storm, cellar doors left open, blown fuses, exposed filaments,
grounded, of this Blue-Ballooned City.

Post-tempest, metalove, I've ended

my liquid diet
of multicolored glass, I've begun

walking from one room
through the others. I've begun turning on

the lights.

The only cure
for Mourning is Time. The only

cure for Time
is Nighttime, the only cure

for Night is
More Night.

For a few lengths we were
enveloped in night,

two inmost coordinates
of its satellites,

splitting each particle
of each other, you and I were

of this
Homesick Sciatic World.

Now from the street I see
the lights inside are shining—

I keep rewiring behind the walls
the Hunger Rooms.

4

ARCHITECTURE

It is Saturday, December 14, 2013.
Today, I will obtain EVIL IN MODERN THOUGHT.
First, I must finish this draft of ARCHITECTURE.
It is snowing. Later, I will walk down three flights
and out the glass entrance. I will obtain
EVIL IN MODERN THOUGHT from X, who taught me
about structure. First, the introduction of a silence:

Good. Four floors above Seventh Avenue,
in Brooklyn, New York, I am drafting ARCHITECTURE.
I have lived here since April. My building
is solid brick with metal venting
fitted through it. I can fold my legs and fit
in the deep sill of the window. I can look out
over the broken land and tower.
In my building, there lives an opera singer.
Sometimes, the vent issues octaves.

Yes, this is ARCHITECTURE. It is for you.
The introduction of a YOU is the introduction
of a structure within ARCHITECTURE.
Let me tell you a story: X is a man who taught me
that enough whiskey between two structures
can erase whatever one may have done to the other.

Let me tell you a story: One day, years back, X
went down three flights and out. (Inconsequence.)
I must not forget EVIL IN MODERN THOUGHT.

DETAIL: I am now folded in the window, overlooking
the broken land and tower. It is snowing still.
You must try again to write the true things.
This was my thinking behind ARCHITECTURE.
The things that happen are the things that happen,
I wrote once. (See THE HOUR OF GREAT CONTEMPT.)
Sometimes, the vent issues arias.

What will I do after ARCHITECTURE?
You kissed me in a restaurant once.
(The YOU is now no longer mere structure.)
ARCHITECTURE is for you, and for the extent
of ARCHITECTURE you are nameless.
Still, you are here, a structure within it. As such,
it holds you. As such, I can hold you.
Now I must leave you here.

THINKING MACHINES

Today I will make a machine called
Thinking Machines. It will be composed of
simple machines. If it goes *think, think,*
we will know that it is working.
If it speaks, I will see the point of speaking.
It is morning. Fellow citizens can see
up from the street the lamplight I work by
casting itself democratically. I take a
hammer to a plank. It's not about emotion.

Here comes a man with his spaniels.
The spaniels are tethered to a leash.
This is the prototype of a desired
quality, one I hope to emulate. At the forge,
I forge his chest, manipulate materials
with gleaming heat. Thinking Machines
will be a working machine. Over
a gleaming screen, he'll bend his
body to the shape of a question.

And this sense of sheer
inconsequence as I monkey-wrench
Thinking Machines together I hope
likewise to install in him. This is Freedom.

Now he is part of something larger.
We are settling down. Now
I am preparing a beast for us to eat.
Across from each other we are
seated, our hands in our laps.

STORIES (II)

It is your last night on Earth.
I am listening to an opera singer from Berlin talk in broken English.
It is a party. From a tumbler glass, I am drinking bourbon,
and she is asking about my poetry.

It is your last night on Earth. I am unaware.
The party is sitting down to dinner. We have switched to wine,
red and white. The opera singer is a friend of a friend of my lover.
He rests his palm on my knee, and I rest my hand on his shoulder.

About my poems, they are less and less about emotion, I tell
the opera singer. A kind of demonstration of how one idea or image
can always follow from the last. *Once there was a man, and then there wasn't,*
I wrote once, remember? You wrote, *I am what is missing.*

Now the party is full and seated on couches.
I drink spirits poured over a single cube of melting ice.
Now, about moving, the opera singer is asking advice.
It is your last night, I am unaware, and have nothing to tell her.

Clarity over emotion, remember. Story over sentiment, you taught me.
I was learning. It is your last night on Earth, and I am sitting there,
drinking spirits poured over a single cube of melting ice. My lover says
tell me when he thinks there's something wrong, I'm learning.

On the last night of your life, of which I was unaware, he said nothing,
and I was off, living mine, with him, my lover, cupping delicate tumblers of ice,
and you were off somewhere between everywhere and nowhere—ice,
ice, ice everywhere—Tomorrow, I would learn it.

During dinner, and after, all the papers were poised to break,
with the dawn, the facts: *Last night was the last night of his life, the great poet,
et cetera.* The party is talking visas and sponsors with the opera singer, who
speaks in broken English.

Why do I speak of this? Because it's easier than saying that
this morning I woke and hid from the light in the shelter
of the broad, living back of my lover, who was sleeping,
asking nothing, commanding nothing.

Once there was a man, and then there wasn't, I wrote once.
This is STORIES (II). It is for you, who are missing. I've kept it poised,
clear, a promise to you, a tribute. It's what you taught me. *Tell me,*
my lover says now, and it's simple, old friend. I cover my face with my hands.

ANTHEM

We are cruel sometimes, and sometimes tender.
To push my hair from my eyes, my lover reaches over.

Not long ago, before we knew each other, we thought
the world was over. I was sixteen, I remember,

and I didn't believe in a soul. It was that September
not so long ago. Regardless, I moved to the city.

There were stars, barely bright, but they were there, and
train-cars carried trapped birds

to the outskirts, and let them go. I didn't understand back then
how or why this life goes, and the stars

seemed to quiver in their static holes. I didn't understand.
I still don't. Now, some nights, my lover reaches over. If we're brave

we call it love, if we're tender. Once, I thought love was over.
Tonight, we climb a ladder. Crowds gather on streets below.

They think the war is over. On the roof, we drink beer,
know better. Once, we thought the city would be the answer.

We thought the stars were souls of those lost long ago. Flocks
of birds burst from trains like clouds of smoke,

and stars were fixed regardless above the ending world.
Tonight, crowds hold up lighters like faith or hope.

The stars are there, but barely. The city wasn't
the answer, but I live here still.

Tell me again, I say, *about the soul,*
and my lover says, *We are made of old stars, remember.*

Tonight, he is tender. To put out the stars, I reach up, to be cruel.
I wanted to believe in something. I wanted to remember it all.

SUNSET DISTRICT

Meet me in the Sunset District, out by the shoreline,
a place named for the time of day that dies. Meet me here
where the gulls are streaked with gasoline, where hubcaps
wash ashore like giant mournful sequins. These days,

from this strip of beach, I watch for hours pairs of lovers
collecting stones, then walking hand in hand
into the ocean. They say the city is dying.
Newspapers, windblown, scatter headlines:

THIS IS IT, they say, WHAT'S DONE
IS DONE, and out here by the sea a man in rags
tries to speak to God on a rotary phone. But meet me
by the dismantling skyscraper that once kept our keys,

that housed this borough's evening sun. From here
we might chance to see vanishing points on the horizon
where troops and artillery wince and glitter
like stolen jewelry. Someday we'll move to the country

of some distant country, but meanwhile, I'll bide my time
watching tides, folding yesterday's paper into airplanes,
whole fleets. Come evening, streetlamps flicker. Streetcars
rear to a halt. A dial tone. *Hello*, I say, *hello?*

So, take your leave and meet me, if you can, the day after
Oblivion. A body in rags will be buried, by then, in black sand.
We'll watch spilt oil rainbow the bay and glint aluminum.
We'll breathe the new air incensed with aftermath and uranium.

AFTER AFTER CATULLUS

Tell the mister
how he'll miss her.

Dismantle those districts,
gone lost, gone sick,

and soothe soothsayers
in distances uneasy,

grease the brakes
in junkyard Corollas,

sparkplugs spent,
pedals like pistils

of ache and feast. So tell
the mister, I say, how

he'll miss her, *The one
he loved, the last*

one left, who sleeps in car-
fuls of careful cut petals,

who stilts and cracks their
wary Stradivarius.

STORIES

Have you heard the one about the man gone missing?
It goes something like, *Once upon a time*, something like,

The man left and left them with nothing. As it happens,
they lost the house that was never theirs. They moved

away, changed their names, and planned to visit the sea. Sometimes,
they'd go driving, nighttime, north to the airport to glimpse

the lights that took flight departing, something like foolhardy stars,
and they named the lights The Floating City. One time,

they drove out, at last, to the sea, traced in sand their new names,
they'd seen how the water couldn't help but darken, wave

after wave, and recede. But in The Floating City, they knew
the lights were lilies luminous in bloom, nothing wilted or

went to waste, no story was erased, and no one would want to leave.
Once upon a time, there was a man. And then there wasn't.

There was The Floating City only they could see, something
else they loved, as it happened, but couldn't reach.

They tried, bound on land, writing their story in tenuous sand,
and it came back to them, breaking again and again.

Someone said, *Nothing lasts.* Someone said, *Something
must happen.* At dusk, they watched their mother plant the poppies

then cover her face with her hands. This one goes out
to the mother in the garden. This one goes out to the brother

driving far from the fleeting sea. This one goes out to
the three of us together. This one goes out to The Floating City.

CONTINGENCIES (II)

Now, my mother has unlearned sleep.
Now, my brother comes to visit, and when he doesn't talk
he sings. Thirty-five, he lives in the Dust Bowl. Twenty-nine,
I live in Brooklyn. You are thirty-two and from far away.

My brother has sacrificed Nearness for Mathematics.
We have sacrificed Rest for Romance. We have our doubts
about the worth of the city. Downstairs,
Vincent's band is playing.

In subway stations, old ads peek through new ones
peeling off: Attempt after Attempt, overlain.
(I wanted to say some PURE and PERFECT thing.) Downstairs,
Vincent's band has stopped playing.

Now, for two friends, with a child on the way, we are viewing
apartments. We stand in one after another. We stood in two
yesterday, and four the day before. You asked as many questions
as you could think of. I stood where strangers had lived and gone.

On our way, we ran into people I used to know in Virginia.
Surprised, everyone smiled, then said *goodbye.*
Now, in the Room of Red Curtains, you are rereading
The Book of Laughter and Forgetting.

A breeze comes in and lifts the red curtains.
We weigh the advantages of going out versus staying in.
We live on the Avenue, just above the space in which we first spoke.
Each night, I call my sleepless mother.

Downstairs, Vincent's band is playing.
His new girlfriend has flown in from Paris, left behind
everything. One night, we see him walking by with his ex-wife:
Battles over, no winner, just calm.

You say that in The Necessary Meaninglessness is The Arbitrary
and therein lies our Freedom. We cook and enjoy our meals.
What rest we enjoy, we enjoy with each other. You say, in your way,
There is no such thing as some PURE and PERFECT thing.

I write: *There is no such thing as some PURE and PERFECT thing.*
For your eyes, it is necessary to spend time
looking far. We sit on a bench on the Avenue.
Sometimes, we see Vincent pass with his new life.

Sometimes, a helicopter circles above and drowns out voices.
We assume it's seeking some desperately missing thing.
(You are the kind of person who gives and gives.)
Other times, we just hear music.

When you are empty, you make a space to read.
Kundera writes: *Man knows he cannot embrace the universe
with its suns and stars.* You sit on a bench
and look far. People walk by, pouring their lives into devices,

and turn the corner. Your eyes contain tiny corrective devices
from a surgery you received, at age eighteen, in Nice.
The doctor's office is in a grand old flat overlooking
the Promenade des Anglais and the Mediterranean Sea.

In my office building in New York, the elevators contain screens
displaying pictures of the sea, in segments called
Monday Morning Ah . . . or *Midday Getaway*, depending.
I ride the elevator up and down at least two times each day.

There is no such thing as some PURE and PERFECT thing.
My brother visits and when he doesn't talk he sings.
Each night, I call my mother from the Room of Red Curtains.
In the kitchen, you cook a meal for us, as you were taught.

I think of you as a boy, with thick glasses, afraid of going blind.
(You are still that boy.) I want to tell you that in Coal Country,
where my grandmother was from, donkeys were plunged
for years in dark mines. To calm them, the boys had learned to sing.

I want to say some PURE and PERFECT thing, but there is
no such thing. How can I apologize to you for the world?
Downstairs, Vincent's band has stopped playing.
Now, it is raining. We lie in the Room of Red Curtains and listen.

Acknowledgments

Many thanks to the editors of the following publications where some of these poems first appeared: *American Chordata*, *BOMB*, *Boston Review*, *Brooklyn Poets*, the *Hide-and-Seek Muse*, *Maggy*, *Paperbag*, *Philadelphia Review of Books*, *Powder Keg*, *Slice*, the *Volta*, *Wave Books Online*, *West Branch*, and *Western Humanities Review*.

Many thanks to my mother and brother. Many thanks to my teachers, especially Lisa Russ Spaar, Mark Strand, Marie Howe, Charles Wright, Rita Dove, Jason Labbe, and Peter Kline. Thank you, Emily Wilson and Mark Levine, for believing in this work. Many thanks to Jerry Shumway. Many thanks to my friends, especially Florencia Varela, Genevieve Burger-Weiser, Greg Atwan, Justin Boening, Danniel Schoonebeek, Libby Burton, and Brittany Perham.

And to Roberto Palomba: I simply cannot thank you enough.